BIBLE STUDIES FOR SMALL GROUPS

Are you together?

DISCOVERING HOW TO RELATE TO THE PEOPLE IN OUR LIVES

by Lance Pierson

Scripture Union, 130 City Road, London EC1V 2NJ
Serendipity (UK), 48 Peterborough Road, London SW6 3EB

Introduction to Serendipity

SERENDIPITY GROUP BIBLE STUDY BOOKS

Serendipity Bible study is essentially a course for small groups, and centres around the growth of relationships in such Bible study groups. It's an approach that helps groups to discover the true meaning of *Koinonia* – a fellowship where people really care and support one another. In each study emphasis is placed on encouraging people to apply God's word in a way that produces action and change and in an atmosphere where there is trust, encouragement and support. In such groups pastoral care develops as a natural consequence of learning together.

The original Serendipity study series was developed in the United States under the authorship of Lyman Coleman. Scripture Union agreed to edit and publish a British edition which is still available from Scripture Union Mail Order: 9–11 Clothier Road, Brislington, Bristol, BS4 5RL.

This current series is brand new – originated in this country and designed specifically for British churches but retaining the essence of Serendipity. If the Serendipity approach is new to you read the section below, *What's behind Serendipity?* This new material has been devised by Serendipity (UK) a recognised offshoot of American Serendipity whose aim is to continue to produce in this country material for study groups wishing to grow not only in their knowledge of God but also in their caring and support for one another.

WHAT'S BEHIND SERENDIPITY?
An understanding of groups

Central to the Serendipity approach is an understanding of how relationships can be nurtured in small groups so that people can learn to take risks in opening themselves to God and to each other. This understanding is best represented by the diamond below, each point of the diamond representing a stage in the life of the group.

People need the opportunity to share something of themselves and need to hear others sharing elements of their own lives, before relationships can begin to open up – this has been called *Storytelling*. Everyone needs to know that they are being listened to, and need encouragement in their

learning and in their relationships. When we respond to someone with a 'thank you', for example, or 'I found your contribution helpful', we are helping them to realise that they are valuable in themselves, and they have a vital contribution to make to the growth of others. This is called *Affirmation*. In experiencing these things in a group that meets together on a regular basis (even over a limited number of weeks) people begin to share their deeper longings or hurts or discover that they can trust others to support them in their struggles. Individuals begin to share what God is saying to them and the changes they need to make in the way they live. This is called *Goal-setting*. Serendipity Bible study material encourages these stages to be reached through Bible study.

Needs in our churches

The needs addressed by this material are reflected in our churches and in society:

1. The need for applied biblical knowledge: Christians are crying out for help in applying their Christian Faith in an increasingly complex world. Knowing what the Bible says isn't enough – people want to know how to translate this knowledge into action.

2. The need to belong: The increased pressures, pace of living, and the constant moving of home, all work against the development of deep relationships. Many feel a need for relationships that are more satisfying, long lasting, and with greater commitment, depth and caring. Some long to belong to a group where there is some stability. Some feel that deeper relationships should be a distinctive feature of the local church as it witnesses to a lonely generation.

3. The need to share the burden: Pressures on Christians as they try to survive in the world are often intolerable – witnessed by emotional/psychological disorders, increased divorce rates and the problems of parenting. Many feel that one answer to this is for Christians to share each others' burdens more seriously – not only prayerfully but in practical ways as well.

4. The need to build the church as a community: a growing conviction that the church is meant to be a community of Christians of all ages and backgrounds who demonstrate in the way they live the true nature of God's Kingdom and who experience what the New Testament means by *Koinonia* or fellowship.

A GUIDE TO THIS SERIES

There are nine books in this series, covering three broad areas of study: **1. A Bible book** (the whole book or a selection); **2. Study of doctrine; 3. Issues in Christian living.** Turn to the back cover for a chart which sets out their titles and subject matter. Each book is self-contained with six or seven weeks' study in each.

HOW TO RUN A SERENDIPITY GROUP

Using Serendipity to form new groups

Serendipity is essentially group study material and, to be used effectively, requires the establishment of *small* groups of people committed to meeting regularly.

Groups of between five and twelve people are ideal for these studies – meeting in someone's home or in a church building. Where groups are larger we recommend that they are sub-divided, each sub-group having its own trained leader. But leave the dividing up until the end of a series of studies, otherwise continuity will be broken. Two or more groups could work independently in the same building in this way.

New people can join groups after a series has been started, but care must be taken in incorporating them. If possible, the leader should meet the newcomer beforehand, to explain what has happened so far. Time can be given at the beginning of group time for the newcomer to introduce themselves to the other members, and vice versa.

Group commitment

Relationships within groups need to be built up and this will only happen if members are prepared to commit themselves to meetings. We recommend that people are asked to make that commitment to the series (six or seven weeks) and then to renew it, if they wish, for further limited periods. In order to emphasise this commitment there is a covenant form in the beginning of each book for members to sign.

Leading a group

Leadership of a small group should not be taken on lightly. Each small group needs a leader who understands Serendipity material, and who has time to prepare and to take responsibility for the practical running of the group. If possible, leaders should attend a Serendipity training course or use the training course provided in *Serendipity Bible studies for small groups: Leader's Guide*. Details of training events, and of this published training course, are available from Serendipity (UK), 48 Peterborough Road, London SW6 3EB.

The leader should feel free to use each session's outline as appropriate to the group – perhaps reducing the time taken over sections or, on occasions, even missing out whole sections. The leader is responsible for seeing that all extra materials are supplied, including extra Bibles.

Worship

Groups may wish to spend much of their time in prayer and worship. Consequently, time-allocation is left to the discretion of the leader who will need to take the group's wishes into account as the session is planned.

Keeping the group open

There is a danger that a small group of people, developing a close relationship between its members, will become inward-looking and isolated from those outside. So it is hoped that groups will make a special effort to 'open their doors' to those around them – friends, neighbours, children of group members, relations etc. Special evenings can be arranged regularly – perhaps every month or every two months – when the programme focuses on a meal, coffee and chat, or on some of the intergenerational 'fun' activities published in the 'families' section of the *Leader's Guide*. You never know – others may want to join your study group as a result of these events!

Using Serendipity in established groups

The Serendipity material can, of course, be used for existing groups. The method is different to many other types of group Bible study, though, and leaders should prepare group members for something different – a different emphasis (application rather than just understanding). Anyone used to one particular form of study is liable to resist a new one, but encourage everyone to participate. Our experience shows that established groups gain far more than they expect to when they use the programme in full. Among the gains for existing groups are: even deeper relationships, the chance for everyone to speak, and the assistance given to leaders especially in terms of helping individuals contribute fully.

Using this series

Each book in this series consists of six or seven studies for groups. Each book is a self-contained course, with leader's notes included. Sessions are designed to be tackled in one evening but they may be spread over two evenings if so desired. Each session is structured in the same way:

Icebreaker (15 mins)

. . . a warm-up exercise at the start of the session to help the group unwind. Usually based around an activity connected with the theme of the session. This section often requires some preparation before the session.

Relational Bible Study (15 mins)

. . . an initial, and fairly light, excursion into the Bible passage, relating it to the lives of those in the group through multiple choice questions.

In-Depth Bible Study (20 mins)

. . . moving deeper into the passage and discovering more about its relationship to life, but sticking to the passage under consideration.

Going Further (15 mins)

. . . an optional section for those who want more depth to their study, often referring the group to other parts of the Bible containing similar teaching. This section may be incorporated into the group time, or offered to group members as homework, or left to those who wish to use it for personal study.

My Story (10 mins)

. . . an encouragement to the group to relate the session's teaching to their lives.

Notes

. . . provide background study material – primarily for those who lead the group – though group members are encouraged to read them, too. Notes on difficult verses, or explanations of the context of the passage, are also given.

Leader's Notes

. . . are given at the back of the book. General points which apply to all sessions are listed. Specific information for each session is also given.

Group Covenant

Before you start on this course, it is important to agree as a group on your goals and common disciplines. Like *Weight Watchers*, the strength of the group is in these common disciplines.

The Covenant

For the duration of this series we agree to the following disciplines as a group:

Attendance: To give priority to the group meetings. Except for emergencies we will be present and on time.

Participation: To give ourselves to the purpose of the group – to get to know each other and become a spiritual community – by sharing our 'stories' with one another.

Confidentiality: To keep anything that is shared strictly confidential.

Accountability: To allow the rest of the group to hold each of us accountable to the goals we set for ourselves.

Support: To give each other the right to call upon one another for help and support in times of temptation and need – even in the middle of the night. We realise that we need the help of each other to overcome temptation, spiritual depression, and weakness.

Evangelism: To be willing and ready at any time to welcome newcomers into the group who need its support and help, and who will agree to these minimum disciplines.

SPECIFICS

We will meet on (day) _____   Babysitting _____

at (place) _____   _____

from (time)_____to _____   Newcomers _____

WHAT WE WANT TO DO ABOUT . . .

Refreshments _____   Absence _____

_____   _____

_____

I will try, with God's help, to be a regular, faithful, caring member of this group.

Signed_____

NAME	PHONE NO.	NAME	PHONE NO.
_____	_____	_____	_____
_____	_____	_____	_____
_____	_____	_____	_____
_____	_____	_____	_____

Remember: new people can join the group at any time during the course.

Are you Together?

Discovering how to relate to the people in our lives.

INTRODUCTION

It is impossible to live daily life without constant interaction with other people. At the most superficial level, there are the people we rub shoulders with – neighbours, the friends we say 'hello' to in the street or on the bus, shop assistants, the person who stops us to ask the way or the time. In addition, many of us share our home with family or friends, and our day with work-mates or children. Each interaction expresses a relationship, and carries potential to develop and deepen it.

These relationships are not simply an accidental fact of life; they are a psychological and emotional need. Unless we have people to talk to, to touch, to share with, we shrivel and wither instead of blossoming and growing. 'God sets the lonely in families' (Psalm 68:6) – indeed, he planned for all of us to be born in them – because we need each other.

If this is true of the human race as a whole, it is no less true of God's new humanity, the church.

A previous generation (in which some of us may have received our Christian upbringing) emphasized personal piety – the individual's relationship with God – to the virtual exclusion of fellowship – our relationship with each other within the Christian community. We have now rightly come to see this as a distortion of Jesus' intention. Alongside the great commandments, 'Love the Lord your God', and 'Love your neighbour as yourself,' he added a *new* commandment, 'Love one another. *As I have loved you*, so you must love one another' (John 13:34). The healthy hunger for right relationships with our fellow-Christians has created the prolific growth of small fellowship groups, such as the one in which you will be using this book. In small groups of four to twelve we can learn the art of giving and receiving love. And unless we learn that, we shall get nowhere as disciples. Jesus himself set the pattern with a small group of twelve.

The 'Serendipity' approach is, we believe, especially helpful in enabling small groups of Christians to discover how to relate to the people in our lives. For one thing, the style of Bible Study is what we call 'relational': it encourages group members to relate or apply the Bible teaching to their own lives, and to share their discoveries with the rest of the group. For another thing, the diamond of group development (see page 2) – whereby each book moves its emphasis session by session from story-telling, through affirmation, to goal-setting – enables groups to build relationships of ever-increasing reality and supportiveness.

The sessions focus on a variety of relationships both inside and outside the church:
1. 'Belonging together' – relationships with those who brought us up.
2. 'Living together' – relationships with the opposite sex.
3. 'Growing up together' – relationships with children.
4. 'Bind us together' – relationships within our church.
5. 'Getting back together' – relationships under strain.
6. 'You've got it together' – using affirmation to keep relationships in good repair.

Each session focuses on our relationships with particular people, draws on skills needed to build and develop the relationships and, within the caring atmosphere of the group, initiates practical action to put the skills to use.

The parallel Serendipity Discipleship book *Look out!* attempts to deepen our account-ability and commitment to other people. This book aims to get us more 'together' in our relationships with them.

Belonging Together

(Leader's notes: pages 29 and 30)

 Aim

To focus on your relationships with those who brought you up; and to share what each group member has inherited from his/her background – both home upbringing and discovery of Christian faith.

 Icebreaker: Family Crest

In the shield below, fill in your family 'coat of arms'. In the left-hand quarters, put two qualities you have inherited from your father; in the right-hand quarters, two qualities inherited from your mother. On the band at the top, write your family 'motto' – try to express in a few words the chief outlook on life that you were brought up to hold; either put it in words of your own, or use a proverb/well known saying/Bible verse, if they express it fully.

 Read: Acts 16:1–3; 2 Timothy 1:5–7; 3:14–17

Acts 16:1–3

Timothy joins Paul and Silas

[1]He came to Derbe and then to Lystra, where a disciple named Timothy lived, whose mother was a Jewess and a believer, but whose father was a Greek. [2]The brothers at Lystra and Iconium spoke well of him. [3]Paul wanted to take him along on the journey, so he circumcised him because of the Jews who lived in that area, for they all knew that his father was a Greek.

2 Timothy 1:5–7

[5]I have been reminded of your sincere faith, which first lived in your grandmother Lois and in your mother Eunice and, I am persuaded, now lives in you also. [6]For this reason I remind you to fan into flame the gift of God, which is in you through the laying on of my hands. [7]For God did not give us a spirit of timidity, but a spirit of power, of love and of self-discipline.

2 Timothy 3:14–17

[14]But as for you, continue in what you have learned and have become convinced of, because you know those from whom you learned it, [15]and how from infancy you have known the holy Scriptures, which are able to make you wise for salvation through faith in Christ Jesus. [16]All Scripture is God-breathed and is useful for teaching, rebuking, correcting and training in righteousness, [17]so that the man of God may be thoroughly equipped for every good work.

 Relational Bible Study

1. Timothy's father and mother came from different races and religions (Acts 16:1). My parents differed in (circle any letters that apply):

a. nationality.
b. part of the country they came from.
c. religious beliefs.
d. political views.
e. ideas on how to bring up children.

6

f. value of money.
g. sense of humour.
h. leisure activities.
i. Other_____

Beside any that you have circled, draw one of these faces to express the effect their differences had on you:

I enjoyed the 😊 variety

It didn't matter 😐 to me.

It made me feel confused insecure/that my loyalties were split. 😖

2. Who was the chief source of 'sincere Christian faith' (2 Timothy 1:5) in your home/family?

a. No-one
b. Grandmother.
c. Mother.
d. Father.
e. Brother/sister.
f. You.
g. Other_____

How did you feel towards that person as a child: hot/warm/normal/cool/cold?

3. When did you first come to know 'the holy scriptures' (2 Timothy 3:15)?

a. Infancy.
b. Later childhood.
c. Teen years.
d. Early adulthood.
e. Middle age.
f. After retirement.
g. Still don't know.

Who was the chief person you learnt from?_____

In-Depth Bible Study

1. What belief/value of your home upbringing do you most strongly agree with?

_____

2. If Paul took me on a missionary journey, I would be good at working with (tick any that apply):

a. children.
b. teenagers.
c. men.
d. women.
e. old people.
f. immigrants.
g. ill/handicapped people.
h. Other_____

Put a cross against any you would not find it easy to work with.
What is it in your home background that influences your strongest tick and cross?

_____

_____

3. Timothy's chief weakness was 'timidity', which God was working to control with 'a spirit of power, of love and of self-discipline' (1:7). Re-write this verse to identify the greatest weakness you have inherited from your background; and to suggest how God wants to build you up to overcome it.

God did not give *me* a spirit of _____,

but a spirit of _____.

4. How are you most aware of God using the Bible in your life (3:15–17)?

a. Making me wise for salvation.
b. Teaching me.
c. Rebuking me.
d. Correcting me.
e. Training me in righteousness.
f. Equipping me for every good work.
g. Other_____
h. Nil.

Going Further

1. Discuss how the following features of Timothy's parental background could have been disadvantageous to him:

    a. One parent a Christian, the other not.

    b. Mother and grandmother Christians, but not father.

How can we be of spiritual help to children with this same background today?

2. Think back over your childhood and teen years.

Think particularly about difficult times, unhappy incidents, bad memories. Do any of these remain with you today – unresolved? Share any of these if it will help and if you are able to, with your group *or* with an individual in your group. If you prefer not to talk about them, offer them to God and seek his continued help and healing.

    Close any time of sharing with prayer (respecting each other's confidentiality), offering what has been shared to God.

My Story

1. Write a short thank-you letter to your parents or those who brought you up (even if they are no longer alive), to express gratitude for the best things in the way they brought you up.

Dear Mum and Dad,

If they are still alive why not post it/read it to them now?

2. Jot down brief notes to help you tell the one or two others in your small group how your faith first 'became sincere', or came alive. Share your 'story' when your group leader gives you the opportunity.

3. Write a short note of appreciation for what each member of your small group has shared about him/herself.

Fill in their names below and, beside each, note one thing you found helpful in what they said. (For instance, you may be glad that Mary said she enjoyed being an only child, because you have only one child yourself; or you may have been challenged by Philip's honesty in saying that he finds the Bible boring, as it stopped you giving a pat answer in your turn.) You may get the chance to say some/all of your appreciations out loud.

NAME:

I am glad you said what you did because:

_____

_____

_____

The earliest reference to Timothy in the New Testament is in Acts 16. It seems probable that he became a Christian on Paul's first missionary visit to Lystra four or five years earlier (Acts 14:6–20). Perhaps Paul took him on to the team as a replacement for young John Mark who had dropped out (Acts 13:13; 15:37–40).

He immediately became one of Paul's closest companions. He worked alongside Paul in Corinth (2 Corinthians 1:19) and on the journey bringing the money collected for the Christians in Jerusalem (Acts 20:4). He frequently joined in the greetings at the beginning or end of Paul's letters (1 Thessalonians 1:1; 2 Thessalonians 1:1; Romans 16:21; Colossians 1:1; Philemon 1:1; Philippians 1:1). He travelled as Paul's representative to Thessalonica (1 Thessalonians 3:2,6) and Corinth (1 Corinthians 4:17); he stayed on as Paul's delegate in Ephesus (1 Timothy 1:3) to establish the young church there. Here it was that he received the two personal letters preserved in the New Testament; the second is probably the last letter on record written by Paul. The bond of affection between the two men was strong; and it is from the personal references in this last letter that we glean comparatively more insight into Timothy's character and background than with most other New Testament personalities.

Acts 16:1
The implication of the Greek phrasing is that Timothy's father had not been a Christian, and was by now dead. (See Howard Marshall's Tyndale commentary on Acts, published by IVP.) In time Paul became like a replacement father to him.

16:2
Good reputation among fellow-Christians is an indispensable qualification for leadership (compare 1 Timothy 3:7,10,13).

16:3
Many Jews would have regarded Timothy as an illegitimate half-caste because of his mixed parentage. His circumcision now was to remove unnecessary obstacles to evangelizing Jews.

2 Timothy 1:5
Paul's emphasis on 'reminding' draws Timothy's attention to his family and spiritual roots, and the reassurance they can provide in times of testing. It is not clear here or in chapter 3 whether Timothy's grandmother and mother became Christians during Paul's visit (ie. probably during Timothy's late childhood/early teens) or earlier.

1:6
Paul (and the elders) laid hands on Timothy when they commissioned him to join the missionary team (see also 1 Timothy 4:14). It was then that he received the spiritual gift necessary to serve God. To remain alight and available to God, our spiritual fires need constant fuelling and stoking.

1:7
Timothy was young and inexperienced. His father had probably not provided him with an adult example of a male Christian (if the deduction from Acts 16:1 above is correct). These two factors, put together, may help explain his natural timidity. Paul instructs the Corinthians not to take advantage of Timothy's timidity, in 1 Corinthians 16:10-11.

3:14
Again, Paul exhorts Timothy to remain true to the spiritual grounding he received as his faith developed. The influences of home and of early Christian teaching upon us are foundational.

3:15
Like all children of devout Jews, Timothy would have imbibed the Old Testament Scriptures with his mother's milk, whether or not she had become a Christian while he was still very young.

3:16
'God-breathed' is the exact translation of Paul's word; it implies that God controlled the Bible's composition to ensure that it contains and communicates what he wants. 'Teaching, rebuking' and 'correcting and training' are probably two pairs of positive and negative opposites, the first referring to what we believe, the second to how we live.

3:17
'Man of God' is a technical, Old Testament term for a prophet, and may particularly refer to Timothy's role as a teacher. It applies more generally to all Christians; no exclusion of women is intended.

Living Together

(Leader's notes: pages 29 and 30)

 Aim

To focus on your relationships with the opposite sex; to celebrate God's creation of the human race as male and female; and to develop sensitivity to the other group members' attitudes to sexuality.

Icebreaker: Almost human?

Which of these animals do you see yourself as being most like?

 Read: Genesis 1:26–31; 2:18–25

Genesis 1:26–31

²⁶Then God said, 'Let us make man in our image, in our likeness, and let them rule over the fish of the sea and the birds of the air, over the livestock, over all the earth, and over all the creatures that move along the ground.'

²⁷So God created man in his own image,
in the image of God he created him;
male and female he created them.

²⁸God blessed them and said to them, 'Be fruitful and increase in number; fill the earth and subdue it. Rule over the fish of the sea and the birds of the air and over every living creature that moves on the ground.'
²⁹Then God said, 'I give you every seed-bearing plant on the face of the whole earth and every tree that has fruit with seed in it. They will be yours for food. ³⁰And to all the beasts of the earth and all the birds of the air and all the creatures that move on the ground – everything that has the breath of life in it – I give every green plant for food.' And it was so. ³¹God saw all that he had made, and it was very good. And there was evening, and there was morning – the sixth day.

Genesis 2:18–25

¹⁸The LORD God said, 'It is not good for the man to be alone. I will make a helper suitable for him.'
¹⁹Now the LORD God had formed out of the ground all the beasts of the field and all the birds of the air. He brought them to the man to see what he would name them; and whatever the man called each living creature, that was its name. ²⁰So the man gave names to all the livestock, the birds of the air and all the beasts of the field.

But for Adam no suitable helper was found. ²¹So the LORD God caused the man to fall into a deep sleep; and while he was sleeping, he took one of the man's ribs and closed up the place with flesh. ²²Then the LORD God made a woman from the rib he had taken out of the man, and he brought her to the man.
²³The man said,

'This is now bone of my bones
and flesh of my flesh;
she shall be called "woman",
for she was taken out of man.'

²⁴For this reason a man will leave his father and mother and be united to his wife, and they will become one flesh.
²⁵The man and his wife were both naked, and they felt no shame.

Relational Bible Study

1 What do you think life would be like if the other sex didn't exist? (Circle any answers that match your reaction.)
 a. Rather fun.
 b. Simpler.
 c. Harder.
 d. Boring.
 e. Frustrating.
 f. Other_____

2. If you had been Adam what would you have said when God introduced Eve to you (2:23)?
 a. Excuse me, this is a 'men only' club.
 b. Your place is in the kitchen.
 c. Darling, we were made for each other.
 d. Well, I suppose she's better than a rhinoceros.
 e. Just what I've been looking for!
 f. Where have you been all my life?
 g. Other _____

3. If you had been Eve, what would have been your first words to Adam?
 a. Well, it's a good job I'm here. You'd never have managed to subdue the earth on your own.
 b. Only Adam? Bit boring, isn't it?
 c. Just a point, dear: God did say 'helper', not 'drudge'.
 d. I know my place – your needs are more important than mine.
 e. I think the tigers would be tamed more easily than you.
 f. I've written out my side of the agreement; you sign here.
 g. Isn't it great! We'll be able to work at this together!
 h. I like your body but I'm interested in your mind as well.
 i. Other_____

In-Depth Bible Study

1. What impression do you get of God's attitude to sex?
 a. We don't talk about it.
 b. Naughty but nice.
 c. Just for procreation.
 d. Very good.
 e. What you do when you're in love.
 f. Only if you're married.
 g. Disgusting.
 h. Other _____

2. Tick which of these qualities you would think it essential to share with a marriage partner. Then grade them in order of importance:
— nationality
— political views
— food likes/dislikes
— social background
— religious faith/philosophy of life
— spare time interests
— intellectual ability
— other _____
— attitude to children
— being in love with each other
— respect for each other
— sexual attraction
— similar age
— sense of belonging to each other

3. Who in this group do you guess is best at:

cooking _____   sewing _____

car-maintenance _____   DIY home improvement_____

electrics/electronics _____   typing _____

knitting _____   gardening _____

caring for the ill_____   flower-arranging _____

Going Further

1. How far is marriage breakdown always attributable to failure in one or more of the three processes in 2:24?
  a. Leave father and mother.
  b. Be united to spouse.
  c. Become one flesh.

2. If God says, 'It is not good for man to be alone' (2:18), why does he leave so many people single for so long? How can we help them, especially if they wish they were married?

3. How would you answer people who say the following?
  a. 'There's nothing wrong with sleeping with any consenting adult, provided you love each other.'
  b. 'You should keep sex for someone you're going to live with faithfully, but there is no need to get married.'

My Story

1. You will NOT be asked to share your answers to this question with anyone else in the group! But God is of course interested in how you feel and would like you to share it with him. Draw one of these faces alongside each aspect listed below of how you cope in living with yourself:

I feel comfortable and am happy with God's provision.

Not sure. Ask me again some time.

I don't cope well and need God's help.

  a. When I am on my own I feel . . .
  b. About my sexuality (maleness/femaleness) I feel . . .
  c. About my body I feel . . .
  d. About my 'marital state' (married/single) I feel . . .
  e. About my relationships with the other sex I feel . . .
  f. About my relationships with my own sex I feel . . .
  g. About close friends I feel . . .

2. This session has made me think about the person God made me.

a. I want to thank God for these features (write them below) of my character and circumstances:

_____

_____

_____

b. I would like to thank these members of the group (write their names below) for what they said/are:

_____

_____

_____

3a. This group (or some members of it) could best help me get myself together in the areas of need this session has focused on, by (tick the way you think would be most helpful):

— praying regularly for me.
— letting me talk it over.
— showing me they love me as I am.
— encouraging me to spend more time with my spouse/family/friends.
— minding their own business.
— other _____

b. Someone in this group I could perhaps help

is: _____

by: _____

NOTES: Genesis 1:26–31; 2:18–25

There are profound truths about human nature to think over here.

1:26–27
The words 'image' and 'likeness' were design terms taken from the building trade. 'Men were placed on earth as God the ruler's statue' (Von Rad), that is the human body is God's construct for revealing his glory. 'God looks at us and sees a reflection of himself' (Luther). There are many ways in which we reflect him, but the two specified here are: (a) active, responsible stewardship of the earth's resources (26); (b) the two sexes, expressing different sides of his character and outgoing love. (This passage is explored more fully in *How Human Can you Get?* Session 2.)

1:28–31
The writer introduces these two activities of sex and work as part of God's *blessing* on the human race; not, as so many have assumed, part of his curse.

2:18,20
'Suitable helper' in English may make the woman sound subordinate to the man. But the Hebrew word is never used in the Old Testament of an inferior; indeed, sixteen times it refers to a *superior*! Here God assigns the woman equal partnership with the man through the word 'suitable', which means 'corresponding to' or 'one who perfectly complements'.

2:19–20
By contrast, Adam demonstrates his superiority over the animals. In Hebrew culture, to give something its name was to assert your authority over it.

2:21–23
Unlike the animals, woman is made of the same stuff as the man; he even shares his name with her. (Hebrew for 'woman' sounds similar to 'man'.) Marriage is designed to include this sensation of *reunion* with 'my other half' – 'we were made for each other'.

2:24
'Being united' includes every level of a married couple's sharing; one home, one family, one 'bank account' (?) as well as one bed. 'Becoming one flesh' stresses their sexual union as the expression and reinforcement of their commitment to each other.

Growing up Together

(Leader's notes: pages 29 and 31)

 Aim

To focus on your relationships with children; to appreciate the high value Jesus sets on childhood; and to encourage the growth of childlike qualities in each other.

 Icebreaker: When I was a child . . .

List some of your childhood favourites, and start re-living some of these memories:

My favourite childhood game: _____

My favourite childhood pet (or animal in the zoo): _____

My favourite childhood hiding place (or place to play): _____

My favourite childhood adult (other than your parents): _____

 Read: Matthew 11:25–27; 18:1–6; 10–14; 19:13–15; 21:14–16

Matthew 11:25–27
Rest for the weary

25At that time Jesus said, 'I praise you, Father, Lord of heaven and earth, because you have hidden these things from the wise and learned, and revealed them to little children. 26Yes, Father, for this was your good pleasure.

27All things have been committed to me by my Father. No one knows the Son except the Father, and no one knows the Father except the Son and those to whom the Son chooses to reveal him.'

Matthew 18:1–6, 10–14
The Greatest in the Kingdom of Heaven

1At that time the disciples came to Jesus and asked, 'Who is the greatest in the kingdom of heaven?'

2He called a little child and had him stand among them. 3And he said: 'I tell you the truth, unless you change and become like little children, you will never enter the kingdom of heaven. 4Therefore, whoever humbles himself like this child is the greatest in the kingdom of heaven. 5And whoever welcomes a little child like this in my name welcomes me.

6But if anyone causes one of these little ones who believe in me to sin, it would be better for him to have a large millstone hung around his neck and to be drowned in the depths of the sea.'

The parable of the Lost Sheep

10 'See that you do not look down on one of these little ones. For I tell you that their angels in heaven always see the face of my Father in heaven.

12 What do you think? If a man owns a hundred sheep, and one of them wanders away, will he not leave the ninety-nine on the hills and go to look for the one that wandered off? 13And if he finds it, I tell you the truth, he is happier about that one sheep than about the ninety-nine that did not wander off. 14In the same way your Father in heaven is not willing that any of these little ones should be lost.'

Matthew 19:13–15
The Little Children and Jesus

13Then little children were brought to Jesus for him to place his hands on them and pray for them. But the disciples rebuked those who brought them.

14Jesus said, 'Let the little children come to me, and do not hinder them, for the kingdom of heaven belongs to such as these.' 15When he had placed his hands on them, he went on from there.

Matthew 21:14-16

¹⁴The blind and the lame came to him at the temple, and he healed them. ¹⁵But when the chief priests and the teachers of the law saw the wonderful things he did and the children shouting in the temple area, 'Hosanna to the Son of David,' they were indignant.

¹⁶'Do you hear what these children are saying?' they asked him.

'Yes,' replied Jesus, 'have you never read,

"From the lips of children and infants you have ordained praise"?'

 ## Relational Bible Study

1. How do you react to Jesus' attitude to children? (Circle any letters that apply.)
  a. He'd have made a marvellous father.
  b. He obviously never had any kids of his own!
  c. He must be talking about 'spiritual children'.
  d. He's biased against adults.
  e. He's too sentimental.
  f. Other_____

2. Mark A (agree), D (disagree) or P (perhaps), to express your reaction to these common opinions about children:
  a. Children should be seen and not heard.
  b. Spare the rod and spoil the child.
  c. School days are the happiest days of your life.
  d. The child is father of the man.

Tick any that you think Jesus would agree with; put a cross by any you think he would disagree with; put a question mark next to any you're not sure about.

3. How do you react to children in general? Test your instincts by where you see yourself fitting into the passages. Put a cross somewhere along the lines, to indicate which of the two opposites your feelings come nearest to:

Children are . . .

(11:25 and 18:3)
to be taught _____ to be learned from

(18:10,12)
to be looked down on _____ to be looked for

(19:13)
to be prayed for and brought to Jesus _____ an interference to important work

(21:15-16)
too immature and undignified to worship God _____ able to praise God perfectly

 ## In-Depth Bible Study

1. You're having an enjoyable chat with another adult, when a child comes to ask you a favour. What would you usually do?
  a. Ignore him and hope he'll go away.
  b. Make him wait till you've finished your conversation.
  c. Smile sweetly but inwardly resent the interruption.
  d. Welcome him as if he were Jesus (18:5).
  e. Other _____

2. How can we humble ourselves like children (18:4)?
  a. Let other people sit in the best chairs.
  b. Enter our second childhood.
  c. Say we're no good at anything.
  d. Never push ourselves forward.
  e. Rely on other people for everything we need.
  f. Trust God without question.
  g. Other _____

3. What childlike qualities do those people have who belong to the kingdom of heaven (19:14)?

a. Innocence.
b. Knowing you're weak and small.
c. Spontaneous directness.
d. Being happy to do what God says because he says so.
e. Trusting God to keep his promises.
f. Soon forgetting grudges.
g. Accepting gifts joyfully.
h. Excitability.
i. Awe and wonder at God's love for you.
j. Lack of self-confident sophistication.
k. Knowing you have no right at all to God's kingdom.
l. Knowing you need help.
m. Other _____

4. Now look round the rest of the group, and put the name of each member against the childlike quality in question 3 that you see most clearly in them. For instance, you might put Jack beside (h) because he is so enthusiastic, and Jill beside (f) because although you often disagree with her, she never holds it against you. It doesn't matter if you put more than one name beside the same quality.

Going Further

1. How might we, even inadvertently, fall into the danger of causing children to sin (18:6)?

2. How effective is your church's pastoral care for children or older young people who appear to lose interest in God (18:12)?

3. What bearing, if any, do 19:13–15 and 21:15–16 have on the age and conditions for baptizing children and welcoming them to communion?

4. In the light of his teaching in these passages, what more could your church family be doing to nurture its children?

My Story

1. 'Your Father in heaven is not willing that any of these little ones should be lost' (18:14). One way I could help to care better for the children who belong to us in this group/church is . . .

_____

_____

_____

2. Now focus on *one* 'child in your life', whom God has made you aware of during this session. It may be a close relation (child, grandchild, nephew, sister, etc.); or a child you have some other special relationship with (godchild, someone you teach, neighbour, penfriend, etc).

Through this child Jesus wants to teach me . . .

_____

_____

_____

To treat this child more like Jesus (18:5), I need to . . .

_____

_____

_____

3. To the 'child' in me (the part of me that is child*like* and may, in some respects, still be child*ish*), Jesus is wanting to (circle the letter that comes closest to what you sense Jesus is feeling for you now; if you know further detail fill it in on the lines):

a. reveal something_____

b. Call me to stand 'in the midst' while he teaches the others something through me

_____

c. Say, 'You are the greatest in the kingdom of heaven'

_____

d. Give assurance that I can't stray too far for him to reach me

_____

e. Shout that he's coming to find me

_____

f. Place his hands on me and pray for me

_____

g. Say, 'I love your praise'

_____

h. Other _____

NOTES: Matthew 11:25–27; 18:1–6; 10–14; 19:13–15; 21:14–16

Jesus was no starry-eyed sentimentalist over what children are really like. He was well aware that they can be sulky and unco-operative (Matthew 11:16–17). But the collection of passages chosen for study summarize his positive teachings about the value of children and childhood. It is a higher view than anyone else has ever put forward, investing children with innate dignity. Each passage reverses one or another popular assessment of children in Jesus' age and in ours.

11:25–27
The paradox here is that children are open to God's revelation, while 'the wise and learned' (the official experts, Pharisees and law-teachers) are not. 'These things', which children perceive (25), seem to refer back to the miracle earlier in the chapter which disclosed Jesus' identity as Messiah (11:3–5, 20–23); and forward to the personal knowledge of God which Jesus his Son mediates (27). As throughout these passages, Jesus uses the term 'children' (25) to illustrate a spiritual condition (27).

18:1–5
The child of verse 2 becomes a visual aid for three startling truths:
- (1.) childlikeness is necessary to enter God's kingdom in the first place (3);
- (2.) childlikeness is the secret of spiritual greatness (1,4);
- (3.) Jesus challenges us to treat children with the same love and respect we would give him (5).

Jesus described the child in front of him as being 'humble' – he was 'nothing' in the eyes of the world: no status, property, money; rather, he was completely dependent on his parents to provide all that he needed.

18:6, 10–14
With graphic pictorial language Jesus stresses God's vigilance in protecting the smallest and weakest in his flock.
- (1.) He warns off those who would corrupt them (6) – 'a *large* millstone' was pulled by an animal, as opposed to the portable, kitchen variety;
- (2.) They are very close to his heart. He always has them in view (10).
- (3.) He personally searches for any who wander away (12).

19:13–15
The disciples may not have been anti-children as such, they may simply have thought Jesus was too preoccupied with his approach to Jerusalem to be delayed. If so, he retorts that he is NEVER too busy for children; they have the right of direct access to his blessing at all times. More than this, he gives them the charter of citizenship in heaven. Indeed, THEY are the archetypal members who show others the way to enter; see 18:3–4 for further explanation of this claim.

21:14–16
The temple authorities were shocked at the lack of ritual purity (the Pharisees usually excluded the blind and lame from the precinct because of their deformity) and of dignity – fancy allowing children to go on carolling bits of the pilgrim psalm AFTER the procession had finished! Jesus hits back at them with a double-edged quotation from Psalm 8:2.
- (1.) It is genuine praise that reaches God, not hypocritical or insincere praise no matter how 'official' the worshippers may be.
- (2.) Implicit in the second half of Psalm 8:2, which Jesus leaves unspoken, is the charge that the temple authorities have become God's enemies.

Bind us Together

(Leader's notes: pages 29 and 31)

 Aim

To focus on your relationships within your own church fellowship; and to explore the family togetherness Jesus intends for his people.

 Icebreaker: The church ice championships

Award your church a score out of six (as in an ice dance championship) for how well it lives up to the ideal expressed in these snatches of songs about the church. Give scores for technical merit ('the letter of the law') and for artistic impression (the beauty of its spirit).

	Technical merit	Artistic Impression
1. 'We are one in the Spirit . . . And they'll know we are Christians By our love . . .'	_____	_____
2. 'We thank you Lord for our life together, To live and move in the love of Christ, Your tenderness which sets us free To serve you with our lives.'	_____	_____
3. 'We're so glad to be your children, gracious Father.'	_____	_____
4. 'Let us lift up holy hands And magnify his name and worship him.'	_____	_____
5. 'The Church's one foundation is Jesus Christ her Lord . . . Her charter of salvation, One Lord, one faith, one birth.'	_____	_____
6. 'In white robes arrayed us, kings and priests made us, And we are reigning in Thee.'	_____	_____
7. 'Like a mighty army Moves the Church of God.'	_____	_____
8. 'Through the night of doubt and sorrow Onward goes the pilgrim band.'	_____	_____
9. 'Go forth and tell! O church of God, awake!'	_____	_____
10. 'Make me a channel of your peace.'	_____	_____

 Read: Mark 3:20–21, 31–35

Jesus and Beelzebub

20Then Jesus entered a house, and again a crowd gathered, so that he and his disciples were not even able to eat. 21When his family heard about this, they went to take charge of him, for they said, 'He is out of his mind.'

Jesus' Mother and Brothers

31Then Jesus' mother and brothers arrived. Standing outside, they sent someone in to call him. 32A crowd was sitting around him, and they told him, 'Your mother and brothers are outside looking for you.'

33'Who are my mother and my brothers?' he asked.

34Then he looked at those seated in a circle around him and said, 'Here are my mother and my brothers! 35Whoever does God's will is my brother and sister and mother.'

Relational Bible Study

1. If Jesus had been your son/brother, what would you have done? (Circle any letters that apply.)
   a. Been proud to have a preacher in the family.
   b. Shrugged it off, hoping he would get over it later.
   c. Gone inside and made a scene.
   d. Told him he was no longer welcome at home.
   e. Gone to see your doctor/minister.
   f. Joined the circle around him.
   g. Suggested he made an appointment with a psychoanalyst.
   h. Followed him around each day with a packed lunch ready.
   i. Other _____

2. In which areas of your life do you feel you are like Jesus' natural family — standing outside the house where he is staying, feeling a bit estranged from him? In which areas of your life do you feel more like those he called his true family — sitting at his feet, learning from him, and doing God's will?
   Put a dot somewhere on the line next to each category, to show which group of people you identify with most closely.

	Right next to Jesus.	At the back of the room.	In the porch.	Outside.	Half-way down the road.
In my family relationships, I'm . . .					
In my main occupation/work, I'm . . .					
In my use of money, I'm . . .					
In my use of spare time, I'm . . .					
In my church commitments, I'm . . .					

3. How do you feel about Jesus wanting to call you brother/sister/mother? Circle any words that express your reactions, then complete the sentence below.

HUMBLED   PUZZLED   EXCITED   UNWORTHY   ROYAL

   HAPPY   LOVED   WORSHIPFUL   POWERFUL

   Other(s)

It makes me want to _____

_____

Read: Mark 10:28–31

28Peter said to him, 'We have left everything to follow you!'

29'I tell you the truth,' Jesus replied, 'no-one who has left home or brothers or sisters or mother or father or children or fields for me and the gospel **30**will fail to receive a hundred times as much in this present age (homes, brothers, sisters, mothers, children and fields – and with them persecutions) and in the age to come, eternal life.

31But many who are first will be last, and the last first.'

In-Depth Bible Study

1. What are you conscious of having 'left' to follow Jesus?

- a. Everything
- b. Home
- c. Family.
- d. A healthy bank balance.
- e. Independence
- f. Ambitions/career.
- g. Nothing.
- h. Other _____

2. What does Jesus mean (verses 29–30) by receiving a hundred times as much?

- a. We're better off as Christians than we would be otherwise.
- b. We are compensated at least a hundredfold for everything we give up.
- c. The blessings outweigh the sacrifices beyond any comparison.
- d. We feel all experiences (persecutions as well as gifts) much more intensely than before we were Christians.
- e. Relationships within the church family can be even deeper and give an even greater sense of belonging than relationships in our natural families.
- f. Other_____

3. See verse 29. Apart from any member of your natural family, who or what in your church fellowship comes closest to giving you the emotional support of:

home (security) _____

brother_____

sister _____

mother_____

father _____

child _____

'fields' (responsibility/work to do)

_____

4. Who in this group have you come to see as making the following contributions to the 'family' of your group?

open home _____

brotherliness _____

parental care _____

childlikeness _____

using livelihood
in God's service _____

enduring persecution/
suffering _____

making us aware of
eternal spiritual
realities _____

Going Further

1. How can we help those suffering tensions because the lifestyle and values of their natural family are different from those of their church family?

2. What form, if any, does persecution for Jesus and the gospel take for you? Are there points at which you avoid persecution by going too softly? If so, what should you do about them?

3. What obstacles are there to your church being a more close-knit spiritual family? How could you overcome them?

My Story

1. (a) One good thing I have received from belonging to this church is . . .

_____

(b) One good thing I have received from belonging to this group is . . .

_____

2. One way we could express our family-togetherness more closely in this church/group is . . .

_____

3. One thing I would like this church/group to give me (eg more support/encouragement, my expenses, a chance to play the organ, a chance to talk) is . . .

_____

NOTES: Mark 3:31–35; 10:28–31

Without mentioning the word 'church', these passages hint at the 'family' basis of the Christian church.

3:31–32
Jesus' mother and brothers did not at this stage understand his mission at all, and had come to take him away (see verse 21). They expected their natural family relationship to have first claim on Jesus' obedience.

3:33–35
But he responds that there is an even deeper obedience to pay (to God's will), and an even deeper family relationship among those committed to it.

10:28
Peter compares the band of apostles favourably with the rich man who has just left Jesus, unable to give up his possessions (verses 21–22).

10:29–30
Jesus underscores the truth that God will let none of his disciples lose out even in this life. But he reminds them that this life is the age of persecutions; we shall only experience the promised blessings in their fullness in the age to come.

10:31
And he prevents any jockeying for position, reward or most favoured status, with the reminder that God's valuation often reverses our expectations.

SESSION 5

Getting back Together

(Leader's notes: pages 29 and 31)

 Aim

To focus on any relationships under strain; and to explore how to repair them.

 Icebreaker: Family aggro

Form groups of four. Take on the roles of a family living together: mother, father, two children. (It doesn't matter if you have to play the part of someone of the other sex.) Now give each member of the family a different one of these personality types:

- Attacker – accuse and blame the others for everything.
- Avoider – try to get out of every responsibility you can.
- Martyr – you always end up doing everyone else's dirty work.
- Peace-maker – the only mature one of the four, seeking to resolve the conflict justly and harmoniously (not necessarily one of the parents).

The scene begins with mother pointing out that the others have all left pieces of washing up undone, despite an agreement that you would share it out evenly. Let things run from there!

 Read: Genesis 32:3–21; 33:1–12

Genesis 32:3–21

3Jacob sent messengers ahead of him to his brother Esau in the land of Seir, the country of Edom. 4He instructed them: 'This is what you are to say to my master Esau: "Your servant Jacob says, I have been staying with Laban and have remained there till now. 5I have cattle and donkeys, sheep and goats, menservants and maidservants. Now I am sending this message to my lord, that I may find favour in your eyes." '

6When the messengers returned to Jacob, they said, 'We went to your brother Esau, and now he is coming to meet you, and four hundred men are with him.'

7In great fear and distress Jacob divided the people who were with him into two groups, and the flocks and herds and camels as well. 8He thought, 'If Esau comes and attacks one group, the group that is left may escape.'

9Then Jacob prayed, 'Oh God of my father Abraham, God of my father Isaac, O LORD, who said to me, "Go back to your country and your relatives, and I will make you prosper," 10I am unworthy of all the kindness and faithfulness you have shown your servant. I had only my staff when I crossed this Jordan, but now I have become two groups. 11Save me, I pray, from the hand of my brother Esau, for I am afraid he will come and attack me, and also the mothers with their children. 12But you have said, "I will surely make you prosper and will make your descendants like the sand of the sea, which cannot be counted." '

13He spent the night there, and from what he had with him he selected a gift for his brother Esau: 14two hundred female goats and twenty male goats, two hundred ewes and twenty rams, 15thirty female camels with their young, forty cows and ten bulls, and twenty female donkeys and ten male donkeys. 16He put them in the care of his servants, each herd by itself, and said to his servants, 'Go ahead of me, and keep some space between the herds.'

17He instructed the one in the lead: 'When my brother Esau meets you and asks, "To whom do you belong, and where are you going, and who owns all these animals in front of you?" 18then you are to say, "They belong to your servant Jacob. They are a gift sent to my lord Esau, and he is coming behind us." '

19He also instructed the second, the third and all the others who followed the herds: 'You are to say the same thing to Esau when you meet him. 20And be sure to say, "Your servant Jacob is coming behind us." ' For he thought, 'I will pacify him with these gifts I am sending on ahead; later, when I see him, perhaps he will receive me.'21 So Jacob's gifts went on ahead of him, but he himself spent the night in the camp.

22

Genesis 33:1–12

Jacob Meets Esau

¹Jacob looked up and there was Esau, coming with his four hundred men; so he divided the children among Leah, Rachel and the two maidservants. ²He put the maidservants and their children in front, Leah and her children, next, and Rachel and Joseph in the rear. ³He himself went on ahead and bowed down to the ground seven times as he approached his brother.

⁴But Esau ran to meet Jacob and embraced him; he threw his arms around his neck and kissed him. And they wept. ⁵Then Esau looked up and saw the women and children. 'Who are these with you?' he asked.

Jacob answered, 'They are the children God has graciously given your servant.'

⁶Then the maidservants and their children approached and bowed down. ⁷Next, Leah and her children came and bowed down. Last of all came Joseph and Rachel, and they too bowed down.

⁸Esau asked, 'What do you mean by all these droves I met?'

'To find favour in your eyes, my lord,' he said.

⁹But Esau said, 'I already have plenty, my brother. Keep what you have for yourself.'

¹⁰'No, please!' said Jacob. 'If I have found favour in your eyes, accept this gift from me. For to see your face is like seeing the face of God, now that you have received me favourably. ¹¹Please accept the present that was brought to you, for God has been gracious to me and I have all I need.' And because Jacob insisted, Esau accepted it.

¹²Then Esau said, 'Let us be on our way; I'll accompany you.'

Relational Bible Study

1. Draw a mood-graph to record Jacob's emotional ups and downs through this story. Put one word/phrase alongside each point you plot to sum up how you think he was feeling then.

EXAMPLE:

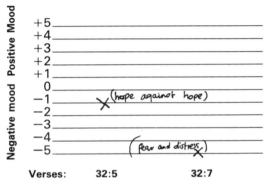

YOUR GRAPH:

(graph with Positive mood +5 to 0 and Negative mood 0 to −5)

VERSES: 32:10   32:12   32:20   33:1   33:3   33:4   33:10

2. The time I felt most like:

Jacob in 32:7–11 was _____

Esau in 33:4–9 was_____

Jacob in 33:10–11 was _____

In-Depth Bible Study

Your answers to the following questions are initially for your own use. There will be an opportunity to share answers, but only those (if any) that you wish to.

1. Is there any member of this group I feel I have

a. misjudged_____

b. thought unkindly of_____

c. envied_____

d. felt threatened by_____

e. got heated with _____

f. argued against unnecessarily _____

g. talked unkindly about_____

h. mistreated in any other way_____

2. Remember Jacob's peace-offerings (32:13–21)! What present would you give, if you could, to help make it up to any person/people listed in question 1?

PERSON   PRESENT

_____   _____

_____   _____

_____   _____

_____   _____

3. On a separate slip of paper, write what you would like to give and say to that person (or to God), in order to make peace. The paper need only be seen by God; it will be offered to him and burnt.

4. Commit each other to God's peace.

Going Further

1. For Jesus' teaching on the activities in this session, read Matthew 5:21–26.

2. For a short, New Testament example of conflict and reconciliation, follow the story of Paul and Mark in Acts 12:25; 13:13; 15:36–40; Philemon 23–24; Colossians 4:10; 2 Timothy 4:9–13. (There is a detailed study of the passages in the Serendipity Youth Bible Study Series book, 'Belonging'.)

3. For a longer New Testament case study of damaged relationships under repair, read 2 Corinthians (with the help of a commentary), especially 1:12–2:4; 6:11–13; 7:2–16; 10:1–11:21; 12:11–13:10. Discuss what light these passages throw on your understanding of this topic.

4. For a study of the qualities required to be a peace-maker within the Christian fellowship, read Ephesians 4:2–3, 15, 25–32. Discuss how these qualities exist in your group/church fellowship.

My Story

1. The person I am most conscious of not being fully at peace with is my:
   a. brother/sister.
   b. spouse.
   c. parent/child.
   d. neighbour.
   e. colleague/work-mate.
   f. boss/assistant.
   g. friend.
   h. fellow-Christian.
   i. Other _____

2. Compared with Jacob and Esau's relationship we are at the stage of:
   a. falling out.
   b. being miles apart.
   c. being out of touch.
   d. God telling me to go back.
   e. thinking about peace offerings.
   f. making first steps towards each other.
   g. embracing and making up.
   h. trying to rebuild.
   i. Other _____

3. What I need to do, in order to move on to the next stage in our relationship, is:

_____

NOTES: Genesis 32:3–21; 33:1–12

The background to the story is this. Esau and Jacob were twins, but at odds with each other from birth, largely because of personality and parental favouritism (25:25–28). Although he was the younger twin, Jacob had cheated Esau of the birthright (25:29–34) reserved especially for the eldest, and of their father's blessing (27:1–40). Esau vowed to kill him, so Jacob fled to his Uncle Laban in Haran, 500 miles away (27:41–44). He stayed there at least fourteen years (29:16–30), till God told him to go home (31:3). And that meant facing Esau.

32:12
Jacob reinforces his prayer with God's own words.

The command in verse 9 quotes 31:3; and this verse claims God's promise in 28:13–15.

33:3
Sevenfold bowing was a sign of homage paid to a king.

33:10
Comparing the sight of Esau's face to God's would, on its own, be a vivid compliment to his brother's free forgiveness, and recognition of God's activity in answering his prayer. But in the full context it is also the echo and achievement of Jacob's mysterious overnight wrestling-match with God (32:24–30).

You've got it Together

(Leader's notes: pages 29, 31 and 32)

 Aim

To focus on your relationships with this group; and to leave them in first-class working order at the end of this course through practice in giving affirmation.

 Icebreaker: Pat on the back

Everyone should have a large sheet of paper stuck on their back, and a felt-tip pen in their hands. Walk round the room, writing two words on each person's back, to express qualities about them which you appreciate (eg 'mature, 'wise', 'fun', 'kind'). You cannot repeat any word that someone else has used.

When everyone has finished, read your paper and savour it. Share the one quality listed that you find most surprising and the one you find most pleasing.

 Read: Philippians 1:3–11

Thanksgiving and Prayer

3I thank my God every time I remember you. 4In all my prayers for all of you, I always pray with joy 5because of your partnership in the gospel from the first day until now, 6being confident of this, that he who began a good work in you will carry it on to completion until the day of Christ Jesus.

7It is right for me to feel this way about all of you, since I have you in my heart; for whether I am in chains or defending and confirming the gospel, all of you share in God's grace with me. 8God can testify how I long for all of you with the affection of Christ Jesus.

9And this is my prayer: that your love may abound more and more in knowledge and depth of insight, 10so that you may be able to discern what is best and may be pure and blameless until the day of Christ, 11filled with the fruit of righteousness that comes through Jesus Christ – to the glory and praise of God.

 Relational Bible Study

In the questions below use Paul's words to help you express what this group course has meant to you.

1. 'Your partnership in the gospel from the first day until now' (verse 5). Doing this course together has deepened my commitment to following Jesus ...

  a. not at all.   c. a lot.
  b. a little.   d. radically.

2. 'All of you share in God's grace with me' (verse 7). Through doing this course together God has blessed me ...

  a. not at all.   c. a lot.
  b. a little.   d. radically.

🔍 In-Depth Bible Study

This time, use Paul's words to express what the other members of the group mean to you.

1. 'I thank my God every every time I remember you' (verse 3). I thank God for this group because . . .

_____

2. 'In all my prayers for all of you, I always pray with joy' (verse 4). My prayer for this group is . . .

_____

3. 'It is right for me to feel this way about all of you, since I have you in my heart' (verse 7). My feelings about this group are:

_____

4. 'God can testify how I long for all of you with the affection of Christ Jesus' (verse 8). Jesus' warm love in me makes me want to say to this group:

_____

📚 Going Further

Affirmation is not just a feature of Serendipity groups; the New Testament is full of it. Paul starts with resounding affirmation in a number of his letters – see Romans 1:8–15; 1 Corinthians 1:4–9; 1 Thessalonians 1:2–10. In the case of the Corinthians, Paul's first purpose in writing is to rebuke (1:10–6:20); but even so he starts by affirming.

Here are some examples of Jesus in action as the Affirmer: Luke 7:9, 24–28, 44–50; 8:48; 10:42; 12:7,32; 18:15–16; 19:9; 21:3–4; 22:15,28–32; 23:43.

So why are we so slow to look for the good in people; to congratulate, compliment and encourage? Think of the things that prevent you, your group, your church, from giving affirmation. Discuss what could help remove any obstacles you identify.

💬 My Story

1. At the end of this course, the chief challenge I believe God is setting before me is . . . (for instance, it may be some responsibility he wants you to take on, some problem he wants you to sort out, some need he wants to meet in you or through you)

_____

_____

2. When you have heard each other's challenge or need, encourage each other by reading and applying verse 6: 'Be confident of this, that he who began a good work in you will carry it on to completion until the day of Jesus Christ.'

3. Then pray for each other, using the words of verses 9–11.
   This is our prayer:
   – that your love may abound more and more in knowledge and depth of insight,
   – so that you may be able to discern what is best
   – and may be pure and blameless till the day of Christ,
   – filled with the fruit of righteousness that comes through Jesus Christ
   – to the glory and praise of God.

NOTES: Philippians 1:3–11

This passage hints that Paul was writing from prison (1:7); later verses make it explicit (12,18). There seems a real possibility that he will be executed (1:20; 2:17). The traditional assumption is that he wrote this while he was awaiting trial in Rome (Acts 28, c. AD 63). In the circumstances, it is all the more remarkable that he starts his letter with praise and prayer so much more concerned for the Philippians than for himself.

Verse 5
'Partnership in the gospel' refers both to their collaboration with Paul in founding and extending the Christian community in Philippi 'from the first day' that he arrived there; and to their financial support

for his later missionary work elsewhere (4:10, 14–18).

Verse 7
God's grace is his love which we go on experiencing, even in adverse conditions; and the ability he gives us to serve him in all circumstances. Paul adds the further thought that it is sharing God's grace together that produces such strong, almost tangible, love for each other.

Verses 9–11
The threefold prayer – for love, knowledge (9) and righteousness (11) – is a perfect general request for spiritual health to use for any Christians, whatever their particular needs.

Special instructions for leaders

GENERAL POINTS TO NOTE

1. Introducing a new course to a group
When starting a new course, spend a few minutes giving the group an overview of the subjects to be covered. Take time to decide how, as a group, you want to organise your meetings (see page 4), and to think about and sign the group covenant. Make sure everyone knows when and where you meet, and how long you meet for.

2. Timing sessions
As a general guide, sections may be timed as follows: ICEBREAKER: 15 mins; RELATIONAL BIBLE STUDY: 15 mins; IN-DEPTH STUDY: 20 mins; GOING FURTHER: 15 mins; MY STORY: 10 mins. For each session, work through the material yourself before the group meeting, checking the timing of each part with the time available to your group.

3. Time for prayer and worship
Your group may wish to spend as much as half the meeting time in prayer and worship. Allow for this in your planning of the session. Always make sure there is time to pray for each other at the end of the session, especially about matters which have been raised during the session. As leader, pray for individuals in the group during the week and as you prepare, and encourage group members to do the same for each other.

4. Giving a lead in sharing
With many of the questions in the sessions it is best to allow time for individuals to fill in their answers for the whole section (eg. 'Relational Bible Study') and then to go around the group sharing the answers. If time is short, or the group is large, pick out only one or two questions in a section for sharing. If people find it difficult to share their thoughts, or are a bit baffled by the exercises which call on their imagination, the leader should go first in sharing.

5. Optional 'Going Further'
'Going Further' is optional. If you do not have enough time for it in the meeting, people may like to work on it at home.

6. Making sure you have enough books
It is wise to have a few spare books for others who might join the group later. It is best if each person has their own book.

7. Leaving an 'empty chair'
Be prepared to integrate newcomers. Introduce them to the group, and the group to them, and make them feel at home.

8. Background notes
The background notes are there for anyone who wishes to know more about the passage being studied. The leader should always read them, and it may be helpful to ask group members to read them through too, either on their own before coming to the session, or together at its start.

NOTES FOR THIS SERIES

Session 1: Belonging together
Aim: People often do not realize how deeply they are influenced by their 'formative years', both physical and spiritual. In general these are positive parts of God's providence, and this session in no way tries to disturb group members' feelings about their past. It aims to give people a chance to talk about their social and spiritual roots; this is an extremely valuable stage of group-building, so encourage an open, trusting atmosphere (perhaps by taking the lead in sharing some of your own answers). You need to be sensitive, though, to any members with an unhappy background, for whom some of these memories may be painful. Err on the side of leaving people free *not* to share their answers publicly in this first session if they would prefer not to.
Icebreaker: Demonstrate how this activity works by giving *your* answers as you introduce it. Most people will find the quarterings quite easy (but be sensitive towards the feelings of those who only know one of their parents). The motto may require more thought; give some typical examples: eg. 'Blood is thicker than water', 'My country right or wrong', 'You shall not steal'. When they are ready ask people to show their crests in twos or threes.

Relational Bible Study: Suggest that people stay in their small groupings – pairs or threes – for sharing throughout the rest of this session. For this study, encourage them to share not just the factual answers, but the memories they evoke.

Going Further: Question 2 is the safety valve in this session for negative experiences of background. Pray for the supportive, healing dimension of your fellowship together; and do everything you can to encourage relationships of complete openness and confidence within the group.

My Story: If your time is short, question 1 may work better as something for people to do at home after the session. Question 2 enables people to talk more fully with their one or two partners about their spiritual beginnings; it is immensely valuable to forming relationships, but you may feel that people have done enough 'baring their souls' for the first session. Question 3 (again limited to the people who have been sharing together throughout the session) is an important conclusion to the proceedings; when people have talked about themselves it is reassuring to learn that others have found it helpful.

Session 2: Living together

Aim: British people, especially Christians, tend to find it difficult to discuss sex. There are some safeguards in the way we have constructed this session; but again, do not force people to share their more personal answers if they do not want to. The session is not about marriage, although married couples should benefit from it incidentally; its aim is more to develop sensitivity to the sexual nature and needs in all of us, especially the unmarried.

Icebreaker: A task similar to Adam's in Genesis 2:19–20! Start with people sharing in clusters of three or four which animal character they most identify with. Then let them have fun relating other members of your full group to the animals; this should lead to general sharing.

Relational Bible Study: Questions 2 and 3: If women find it impossible to imagine themselves as Adam (Question 2) or men as Eve (Question 3), ask them to answer the question as if they were the man or woman they know best (husband/wife, father/mother, boyfriend/girlfriend, brother/sister).

In-Depth Bible Study: Question 3 – a chance to explore sexual stereotypes, and learn more about each other in the process. Start with everyone guessing who are the group's experts at traditionally male/female pursuits. Then share generally who sees each activity as one of his/her specialities (don't worry about deciding who is *best*). Note any 'surprises' (eg. male knitters and sewers – watch how you pronounce this last word!); and note any skills that could contribute to the life of the group and church. If you wish to spend more time on this topic the group could discuss the way they *do* stereotype the sexes, and how this may be a help or a hindrance to relationships between the sexes (inside and outside the church).

My Story: Question 1 – Again, assure the group that no one is required to share their answers with anyone other than God. However, many people may well find it helpful to talk further with someone sympathetic; either yourself or other pastoral carers within your church. Questions 2 and 3 can also be answered alone and followed with silent prayer; but they offer the chance to open up further sharing within the group. Your fellowship will deepen, the more you can thank each other and ask for each other's help like this.

Session 3: Growing up together

Aim: 'In order to know a person truly, you need to see them with children' (Margaret Evening, *Who Walk Alone*, Hodder & Stoughton 1974, p. 153). This session is primarily about how we relate to children and to the child who still lives in each one of us. The focus is not particularly on members of the group who are parents of young children; though naturally they will benefit greatly from it, and contribute greatly to it. If some people find 'childhood' too big a period for simple answers, suggest they pinpoint the age of eight or nine.

If group members find it difficult to see the relevance of a study on childhood, remind them of the special place Jesus gave to children in relation to the kingdom.

Icebreaker: Share answers in small groups of three or four at the most. Encourage people to talk about the feelings these memories recall; you will have difficulty stopping them!

Relational Bible Study: Question 3 – be ready to share your own answers to help people know how to tackle this question.

In-Depth Bible Study: This is a simple opportunity for 'affirmation'. Group members build each other up by appreciating out loud something positive and valuable in each other. If this might be too awkward still in the full circle, share answers in small groups of three or four, to get people in the practice of affirming, but without always giving it face-to-face.

Going Further: Be sure to pass on to your church leadership any criticisms or suggestions that emerge from this discussion.

My Story: Encourage people to take time to reflect deeply on these questions. Questions 1 and 2 – share answers as a basis to praying for each other. You may want to leave question 3 without sharing; but it will be enormously enriching if you feel you are committed enough to each other to share in either of two ways: (i) when one person has shared what (s)he thinks Jesus wants to say or do, the rest of the group should put it into words or actions by, for example, suggesting what he wants to reveal, or laying on hands and praying; (ii) You can increase the affirmation element by answering the question for *each other* rather than for yourself (eg Jack says, 'I think Jesus wants to say to the child in Jill, "Don't worry that God seems far away at the moment; he'll not let you stray far from him." ').

Session 4: Bind us together

Aim: This session explicitly attempts to deepen relationships among your group members. In particular, it aims to widen the focus to include relationships with others in your church family. The main method used is affirmation as explained in 'An understanding of groups' on p. 2.

Icebreaker: It is all too easy to be negatively critical. So encourage people to share only the songs on which they awarded your church the *highest* score; and to suggest how that feature of the church life could improve still further. Pass on ideas, and especially any appreciative comments, to your church leadership.

In-Depth Bible Study: Question 4 – This is the most direct and personal form of affirmation in that each member names who they see as most gifted by God in different aspects of discipleship. It runs the risk that some people may not get named at all. If you feel that your group is not yet ready to share this level of openness in the full circle, ask people to compare answers in pairs.

Going Further: Be sensitive to any feeling distress, and give them time to talk if they need it.

My Story: Questions 2 and 3 – either decide in advance whether to focus these questions on the group itself, or on the wider church fellowship; or let each member choose for themselves. Question 3 – do everything you can to give each member what they ask for *as soon as possible* – preferably on the spot!

Session 5: Getting back together

Before the session: Decide very carefully which sections you plan to include; if In-Depth Bible Study, prepare a separate slip of paper for each person.

Icebreaker: Groups of three will work equally well; simply omit the Avoider. Let the 'family row' run for about five minutes, then call a halt. Ask people to discuss what the conflict felt like, and how far the Peace-maker succeeded in resolving it. How close was it to group-members' experience?

Read: Before reading the set passage, fill in the background by referring to the first paragraph of the Notes on page 25.

In-Depth Bible Study: This is slightly different from usual; sharing of answers is entirely up to the individual. It gives a chance for group members to hand over to God any sore relationships among each other. It is especially suitable if you are in the practice of sharing communion together as a group. But it needs sensitive handling and if you do not feel confident about it you would do better to replace it with one of the study passages in Going Further.

Question 3 – collect the slips of paper, place them on a baking tray and set fire to them in full sight of the group. As you do so, assure them that God forgives our sins, removes any barrier to peace between us, accepts our tokens of repentance, and fills us with his love for each other. Perhaps accompany the flames with a reading of a few Bible verses, such as Hebrews 12:28-29; Psalm 103:12; Ephesians 2:13-18; 2 Corinthians 7:9-11; 1 John 1: 6-7; 3:14.

Question 4 – structure this as is most appropriate for your group. If you are celebrating the Lord's Supper, it will be a natural part of the worship. You may want members to use a formal greeting to each other ('The peace of the Lord be with you'), to help them put into words what they would otherwise find hard to express. Or you may prefer a more informal mingling and sharing of news and needs. Or it might work better as a session of prayer for each other. The section of the Bible passage which suggested this response is 33:4; your group may be able to express love through an embrace, kiss or tears, but never attempt to force this, if it is not natural. Similarly, it may be appropriate to suggest that people use this opportunity to apologize privately for ways they have offended other members of the group, and/or to give their (real or token) peace-offerings. But do stress that it is only helpful to confess to 'visible' sins of word or deed; to start admitting bitter thoughts towards unknowing victims usually just stirs up further recriminations!

My Story: This is a thorough example of goal-setting. Each group member should focus on the relationship in their life most in need of repair, and then on what practical step they could take to help make peace within the next few days. The group should pray specifically for each other at the end, and start the next session by hearing progress reports.

Session 6: You've got it together

Progress: Don't forget at some stage to ask for progress reports on the peace-making goals people set for themselves at the end of Session 5.

Aim: This session brings the course to a close by (1) helping people look back and sum up what it has meant to them; (2) letting the focus finally rest on the relationships with each other in the group; (3) giving further and fuller expression to affirmation as the way to build relationships in love; (4) ending with prayerful, committed support for each member as they set personal goals.

The timing for some parts of the session is slightly different from normal, as detailed below, to make room for these emphases.

Icebreaker: If people find it hard to affirm qualities, they may also include skills (eg good guitar-player, cake-baker, Bible study leader). And while they should not repeat *words* already listed, they may find variants of the same concept (eg kind, generous, self-sacrificing).

Relational Bible Study: 10 mins only. As always, the value in sharing these questions will not be the bare answer, but the explanation of it.

In-Depth Bible Study: 15 mins only. Some people may find it hard to put their feelings into words. Enable them to draw instead, if that comes more naturally, on the page or on a balloon. When it comes to sharing answers, some may be able to express more by touch, kiss or hug than by words; if this way of demonstrating affection is difficult in your group, you could offer people a cuddly toy to *represent* the group ('do to this teddy what you'd like to do to us!').

My Story: 20 mins. This takes the form of a small act of commissioning. It would be appropriate to combine it with communion, if this is normal practice in your group. The sequence is: (1) one person shares and explains their challenge/need; (2) someone else in the group/sub-group responds by reading the encouraging words of verse 6, if possible expanding and applying it (eg 'Over these last six weeks I have seen God at work making you more patient, and I believe that as he carries on doing this, you will find his resources to cope with your sick mother.'); (3) the first person kneels in the centre of the circle, and either one person or the whole group lay hands on his/her head and prays the prayer of verses 9–11 aloud, with special reference to the particular need. They may like to write the application given to them in the space after question 2. Then it is someone else's turn to share and be commissioned.

Reprinted: July 1988